Grand Teton National Park

John Hamilton

Published by ABDO Publishing Company, 8000 West 78th Street, Suite 310, Edina, MN 55439.
Copyright ©2009 by Abdo Consulting Group, Inc. International copyrights reserved in all countries.
No part of this book may be reproduced in any form without written permission from the publisher.
ABDO & Daughters™ is a trademark and logo of ABDO Publishing Company.

Printed in the United States.

Editor: Sue Hamilton
Graphic Design: John Hamilton
All photos and illustrations by the author, except p. 12 Jedediah Smith, courtesy Washington Secretary
of State; p. 13 map, National Park Service; p. 14 John D. Rockefeller, Jr., National Park Service;
p. 18 pika, courtesy Justin Johnsen; p. 20 coyote, Comstock; p. 22 elk, Comstock; p. 24 (top) bald eagle,
Comstock; p. 24 (bottom) grizzly bear, Comstock; p. 26 moose, United States Army.

Library of Congress Cataloging-in-Publication Data

Hamilton, John, 1959-
  Grand Teton National Park / John Hamilton.
      p. cm. -- (National parks)
  Includes index.
  ISBN 978-1-60453-092-6
  1. Grand Teton National Park (Wyo.)--Juvenile literature. I. Title.

F767.T3H36 2009
978.7'55--dc22
                          2008011890

Contents

Left: A horse corral in Mormon Row, a collection of pioneer buildings preserved by the National Park Service.

A pioneer-era barn in Jackson Hole, with **Grand Teton** looming behind.

Mountain Majesty

Think of Grand Teton National Park, and you think of mountains. The Teton Range, for which the park is named, is a classic Rocky Mountain icon, stretching north and south along the northwest corner of Wyoming. This is how mountains *should* look. They rise up suddenly from the valley floor. No foothills obscure the view of their rocky summits, which gnash the sky like jagged teeth. Their classic pyramid shapes come from centuries of erosion caused by glaciers, a process that continues today.

Five alpine peaks dominate the mountain range: Grand Teton, Middle Teton, South Teton, Mount Owen, and Teewinot Mountain. Several other giants rest shoulder-to-shoulder with these five, creating an alpine barrier called the Cathedral Group, one of the most famous vistas in the West.

Tallest of the Cathedral Group is Grand Teton, called "The Grand" by local people. It reaches a dizzying height of 13,770 feet (4,197 m) above sea level. Nearly 7,000 vertical feet (2,134 m) separate the valley floor from the tip of The Grand's summit. It is the highest mountain in the park, and the second highest in Wyoming (behind 13,804-foot (4,207-m) Gannett Peak). Mountaineers crane their necks upward, irresistibly drawn to The Grand's spire, declaring, "I must climb that." Each year, hundreds of people scramble to the summit, an achievement that usually takes two days.

Cathedral Group

If the mountains were the only attraction of Grand Teton National Park, it would be enough. But it has so much more to offer. The list of outdoor activities is long: camping, fishing, cross-country skiing, boating, and more. There are over 200 miles (322 km) of trails for hikers and backpackers to enjoy.

Wildlife viewing is always popular. Tiny pikas live in the high country, while herds of elk wander the forests and meadows. Deer, pronghorns, moose, coyotes, bears, and buffalo are often spotted by lucky visitors. Elusive wolves are harder to spy, but their eerie howls are sometimes heard echoing through the forests.

The majority of the park's 2.5 million annual visitors are not climbers. They are perfectly happy to park their cars and take pictures of the mountains from the sprawling flat valley called Jackson Hole. Twisting through the green, sagebrush-covered Jackson Hole is the Snake River, plus its tributaries flowing off the mountains. Lodgepole pine forests grow on the lower elevations. Blue ponds and trout-filled lakes dot the landscape. The biggest, Jackson Lake, is immense, plunging to a maximum depth of 438 feet (134 m). Smaller, but no less impressive, is Jenny Lake, nestled against the mountains like a blue jewel. Many people make the famous lodges and campgrounds along the shores of these two lakes their base camps for exploring Grand Teton. Others stay in nearby Jackson, Wyoming, a bustling town proud of its Western roots.

Oxbow Bend is a scenic portion of the Snake River running through Jackson Hole in front of the Teton Range. Mount Moran is reflected in the water.

A bison wanders along the flatlands of **Jackson Hole.**

Mountain Geology

Grant Teton National Park rests in the northwest corner of Wyoming, just south of Yellowstone National Park. It is surrounded by national forests and other federal lands run by the Forest Service. To Grand Teton's west is the Idaho border.

Dominating the park is a string of mountains called the Teton Range. These are the youngest set of peaks in the Rocky Mountains. Millions of years ago, there was nothing here but an inland sea. Starting about 13 to 17 million years ago, seismic activity—earthquakes—along the Teton Fault caused two huge blocks of the earth's crust to shift. Like the swinging doors of an Old West saloon, one block tilted skyward, forming the mountains. The other block moved down, creating the valley of Jackson Hole.

The shape of the mountains we see today was caused by the powerful erosion of glaciers. Rivers of ice, some as thick as 3,000 feet (914 m), slowly carved the mountains, depositing massive amounts of debris into the valley. After the last ice age, smaller mountain glaciers, some of which exist today, carved the jagged peaks and created the beautiful chain of lakes at the mountains' base.

Even today, erosion continues to change the Tetons. Glaciers and landslides alter the landscape slightly each year. The Snake River, which starts in the southern part of Yellowstone National Park, winds through Jackson Hole, cutting it in half lengthwise. Year after year, debris from the valley is slowly washed away, eventually making its way to the Pacific Ocean. Meltwater from the surrounding mountains empties into the Snake River, creating a network of wetlands that is rich habitat for wildlife, trees, and plants.

Grand Teton and Teewinot Mountain (left) loom over Jackson Lake.

"The mountains are calling and I must go"

—John Muir *(Above: Grand Teton (right) after a late-afternoon thunderstorm.)*

History in the Park

Humans first came to the Jackson Hole area about 11,000 years ago, shortly after the last ice age glacier had retreated from the valley floor. These early people were hunter-gatherers, collecting plants and hunting animals such as bison and mule deer. Later, several Native American groups, such as the Shoshone tribe, continued using the area as a source of food. People seldom lived here year-round, however, because of the long, harsh winters.

In the early 1800s, mountain men ventured into the Jackson Hole area. These fur trappers and traders were drawn to the Rocky Mountains by valuable beaver pelts, which were used mainly to make hats back East and in Europe. John Colter, a

Jedediah Smith

veteran of the Lewis and Clark expedition, may have been the first white person to see the Tetons, in 1807. Famous mountain man Jedediah Smith also spent time in the area. David "Davey" Jackson found early success trapping beavers. Fellow trappers named Jackson Hole after him. (A "hole" is a flat valley surrounded by mountains.) Soon, other trappers entered Jackson Hole, many of them working for Manuel Lisa's Missouri Fur Company, Jim Bridger's Rocky Mountain Fur Company, and John Jacob Astor's American Fur Company.

By 1840, the beaver trade collapsed, thanks to over-trapping and changes in fashion. The Jackson Hole area was quiet for the next 30 years, as pioneers bypassed the rugged terrain on their way to Oregon, or the gold fields of California.

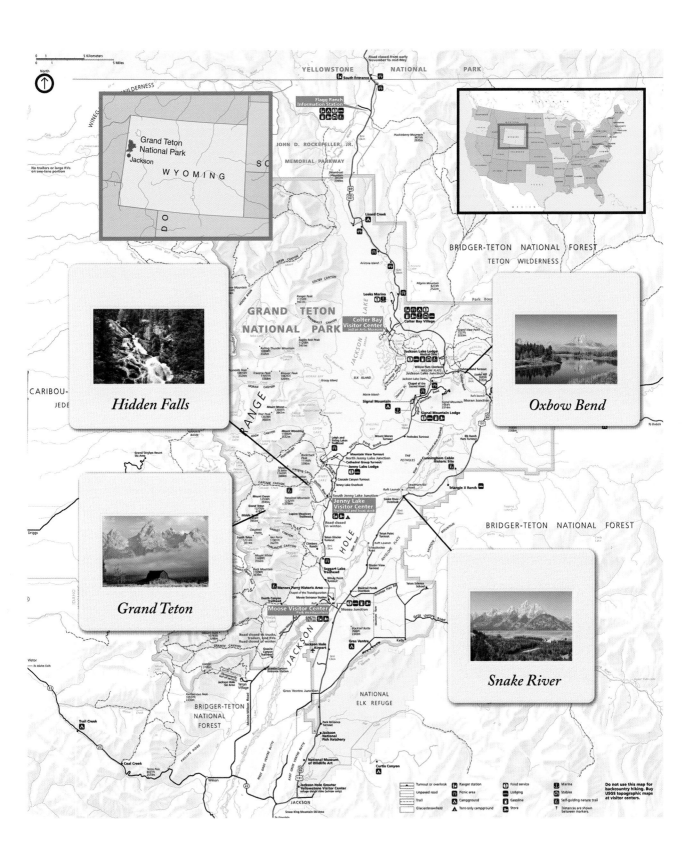

Hidden Falls

Oxbow Bend

Grand Teton

Snake River

In the 1870s and 1880s, farmers and cattle ranchers began settling in Jackson Hole. They became the first full-time residents, lured to the area by the promise of free land from the federal government. The Homestead Act of 1862 gave settlers 160 acres (65 ha) of land if they agreed to live there for at least five years.

J. Pierce Cunningham's story is typical of many Jackson Hole homesteaders. The 20-year-old New Yorker came out West in 1885. He spent the next few years trapping, but around 1890 he and his new wife staked a claim just south of Spread Creek, overlooking the Snake River. He raised cattle, which was difficult because of the area's long, bitterly cold winters. For shelter, Cunningham built a "dogtrot"-style log cabin, which had two small rooms built side-by-side with a covered breezeway in the middle. The cabin exists today, and is a popular attraction in the park.

By the late 1890s, people began to propose ways to preserve the natural beauty of Jackson Hole and the Tetons. The United States Congress in 1929 created Grand Teton National Park, but it only included some of the mountains and nearby lakes. In 1943, President Franklin Roosevelt approved setting aside additional land, which would be called Jackson Hole National Monument. Ranchers and other local people strongly opposed the park because it hurt their livelihoods. After World War II, however, many of these people realized that tourism was the future of the area. Finally, in 1950, the original park boundary was combined with the national monument, plus thousands of acres of private land donated by billionaire John D. Rockefeller, Jr. The current Grand Teton National Park now includes approximately 310,000 acres (125,453 ha) of stunning parkland for all to enjoy.

Left: John D. Rockefeller, Jr., and his wife, Abby, at Jackson Hole National Park. Rockefeller was very active in buying and setting aside land for several national parks, including Grand Teton. The John D. Rockefeller, Jr., Memorial Parkway between Grand Teton and Yellowstone National Parks is named in his honor.

Purple thistles growing in front of the **Cunningham Cabin.**

A panoramic view of the Tetons and Jackson Hole (above). The Cathedral Group (below), including Grand Teton, center, looms over a pioneer settlement called Mormon Row.

The outskirts of Jackson, Wyoming, after a late-afternoon thunderstorm (below). The view is from Teton Pass, south of the park, looking northeast into the valley of Jackson Hole.

Alpine Ecosystem

The ecosystem that Grand Teton National Park is most famous for is its alpine zone. The air here is thin and bitterly cold. It is impossible for trees to grow on the barren rock, which is why the alpine zone is called "above treeline." There are more than 12 peaks in the park that are taller than 12,000 feet (3,658 m).

Winters in alpine ecosystems are long and harsh. Snow covers all but the steepest cliffs. Summers are brief. Naturally, it is difficult for life to find a foothold in such extreme conditions, but if you look closely, you can find a thriving alpine community.

Lichens and moss, resistant to the cold and wind, cling to the rocks. Many insects live in the high country, which attract hungry white-crowned sparrows. Larger animals live here, too. Pikas look like large hamsters, but are related to rabbits. They are sometimes called "whistling hares" because of the shrill peep they make when alarmed. Yellow-bellied marmots are rodents that are found in alpine zones all over the world. These large ground squirrels are often spotted sunning themselves on the rocks. Predators, such as hawks and weasels, often prey on pikas and marmots. During winter, most of these animals either hibernate or retreat to warmer, lower elevations.

Pika

More than 176 inches (447 cm) of snow blankets the mountains in winter. In the summer, most of it melts away by July, but some snowfields remain. These permanent glaciers look small when seen from the valley, but they are actually quite large. Over thousands of years, the masses of ice continually scour the surface of the mountains, forming the jagged peaks and ridges we see today.

Glaciers drape the north face of **Mount Moran.**

Sagebrush Flats

Resting under the Teton Range are the sagebrush flats of Jackson Hole. Sagebrush is a kind of plant that is found in many places in the West. Silvery- or gray-green in color, with yellow flowers, sagebrush is a shrub that thrives in thin, rocky soil. It has a strong, pungent odor, especially when wet. Sagebrush doesn't need much water to live. It covers much of Jackson Hole, along with more than 20 kinds of other hardy grasses and shrubs.

Sagebrush flats look sparse, almost desert-like. Surprisingly, there is a diverse amount of wildlife that lives here. Many kinds of birds, such as sage grouse and meadowlarks, use the plants as shelter. They make their nests in the underbrush, hidden from predators. They also find abundant food among the grasses.

Ground squirrels, deer mice, and chipmunks skitter across the ground, searching for food. High above, raptors such as red-tailed hawks keep a watchful eye for an easy meal. Larger mammals, such as bison, badgers, coyotes, and wolves, also make their homes in Jackson Hole. In summer, pronghorns migrate to the valley. A type of antelope, these deer-like creatures can run up to 70 miles per hour (113 kph). They retreat south in winter to avoid the deep snows.

Left: Coyotes stalk small mammals, such as rabbits, mice, and chipmunks, on Grand Teton's sagebrush flats.

Sagebrush flats dominate the landscape of **Jackson Hole.**

Like pronghorn, elk make their summer home in Jackson Hole. In fact, the area is famous for its herds of these large members of the deer family. Elk are often seen venturing into the sagebrush flats in the mornings and evenings, feeding on the grasses. In winter, 7,000 to 8,000 elk come down off the high country to live in the National Elk Refuge, a 24,700-acre (9,996 ha) sanctuary south of the park.

Elk

The great majority of Grand Teton National Park's visitors see the mountains from two roads that wind through Jackson Hole. Highway 89 closely follows the Snake River. There are many places to stop for superb views of the mountains, which loom to the west. The alternative is Teton Park Road, which runs close to the base of the Teton Range. The newly opened Craig Thomas Discovery and Visitor Center is on this road, just a short drive from the nearby town of Jackson, Wyoming.

Just up the road from the visitor center is Menor's Ferry Historic Area, a collection of pioneer-era cabins and other buildings. A working pontoon ferry takes visitors across the Snake River, the same way early settlers got from one side to the other. Pioneers paid fifty cents to cross the river; visitors today ride for free.

Left: A park ranger operates the ferry crossing the Snake River at Menor's Ferry Historic Area.

The Snake River (above) winds its way through Jackson Hole beneath the Teton Range.
A 1905 store (below) is one of several pioneer buildings preserved at Menor's Ferry.

Forests

Bald Eagle

Lodgepole pine forests drape the shoulders of the Teton Range. These dark-green forests also dot the valley of Jackson Hole in places where tree roots can find adequate water, such as near the Snake River or its tributaries. Lodgepole pine trunks are long and straight. They were valued by early pioneers for making cabins and other buildings. Native Americans used the trees for tipi poles. On drier mountain slopes, Douglas fir thrives up to an elevation of about 8,000 feet (2,438 m).

Lodgepole forests are important sources of shelter for many animals. Elk and mule deer wander into the forest during midday to escape the summer sun. Black and grizzly bears forage in the woods for insects and berries. Red squirrels and deer mice also live in the forest, always on the lookout for weasels and red-tailed hawks. Bald eagles like to perch on tree branches overlooking rivers and lakes, scanning the water for fish. Great horned owls hunt for mice and gophers.

Grizzly Bear

Many people are content to drive through Grand Teton National Park, getting out of their cars only occasionally to take pictures of mountain vistas. But there are more than 200 miles (322 km) of hiking paths in the park. Many of them are easy strolls, passing through majestic forests. Walk just a little ways beyond the beaten path, and it's like you have the entire park to yourself. If you're lucky, you may hear the distant bugling of a bull elk or a howling wolf. It's an experience not to be missed.

Hidden Falls is a short distance from Jenny Lake up Cascade Canyon.

Lakes and Wetlands

There are more than 100 backcountry lakes in Grand Teton National Park. The park's jewels, however, are the big lakes at the base of the mountains, including Jackson Lake, Leigh Lake, and Jenny Lake. These were all formed by glacial moraines. Thousands of years ago, ice-age glaciers ground their way down the mountains, carrying massive amounts of rock, gravel, and other debris. After the glaciers finally melted, the debris acted as a dam, or moraine, which trapped lakewater between them and the base of the mountains.

Today, Jackson Lake is the biggest lake in the park, covering more than 25,000 acres (10,117 ha). Beautiful Jenny Lake, though smaller, is a highlight for many park visitors. A path wraps around the lake's entire 6.6-mile (10.6 km) shoreline. To save time, shuttle boats regularly whisk people across the cool waters. From the far shore, hikers can venture a short distance up Cascade Canyon to view Inspiration Point and Hidden Falls.

Grand Teton National Park has a rich variety of wetland habitats. The Snake River and its tributaries shelter many kinds of birds and animals. Moose are often spotted browsing shallow water for tender plants. Sharing the wetlands with these giants are river otters, pelicans, and blue herons. Coursing through the park's rivers and lakes are native cutthroat trout, rainbow trout, and other fish.

Moose

Boaters enjoy the cool waters of beautiful **Jenny Lake.**

Future Challenges

Grand Teton National Park has always balanced an uneasy relationship between those who want to preserve the area's natural beauty and people who depend on the land for their livelihoods, like ranchers and real-estate developers. In the early 1900s, there was great local resistance to setting aside Jackson Hole as a national park. In 1919, Yellowstone National Park Superintendent Horace Albright traveled to Jackson, Wyoming, to promote his idea of enlarging Yellowstone to include portions of the Teton Range. He was practically "run out of town" by angry ranchers.

After Grand Teton National Park's establishment in its present boundaries in 1950, people have slowly come to realize the importance of preserving natural areas for future generations. Besides this lofty goal, they also understand that there is a lot of money to be made catering to the 2.5 million visitors who flock to the area each year. The crush of tourists, however, brings its own set of problems.

Left: Increased tourism means that park rangers are kept busy with crowd control and other law enforcement responsibilities.

Jackson Hole Airport is the only commercial airport that is inside a national park. It is a busy airport; in 2006, more than 275,000 people arrived, most of them on large, commercial jets. Environmentalists worry not only about the noise (which affects wildlife), but also about the increased number of people using park resources. On many summer days, popular parts of the park can be very overcrowded, especially the area around Jenny Lake. Park officials are studying ways to reduce the number of cars in key spots around the park. This might involve the use of shuttle busses, a system that has worked well in Arizona's Grand Canyon and Utah's Zion National Parks.

Another problem that worries park officials is the introduction of non-native species that compete with the area's original inhabitants. Exotic species found in the park include the New Zealand mud snail, the zebra mussel, many types of noxious weeds, and several kinds of fish. The Forest Service continues its effort to control the spread of damage when non-native species invade the park. Control efforts include spraying, using natural predators, and educating the public about the problem.

Above: Jackson Hole Airport is the only commercial airport inside a national park.

Glossary

Alpine

In high mountains, alpine is the vegetation zone above the treeline, where it is too cold for trees to grow.

Ecosystem

A biological community of animals, plants, and bacteria, all of whom live together in the same physical or chemical environment.

Federal Lands

Much of America's land, especially in the western part of the country, is maintained by the United States federal government. These are public lands owned by all U.S. citizens. There are many kinds of federal lands. National parks, like Grand Teton National Park, are federal lands that are set aside so that they can be preserved. Other federal lands, such as national forests or national grasslands, are used in many different ways, including logging, ranching, and mining. Much of the land surrounding Grand Teton National Park is maintained by the government, including several national forests and wildlife refuges.

Forest Service

The United States Department of Agriculture (USDA) Forest Service was started in 1905 to manage public lands in national forests and grasslands. The Forest Service today oversees an area of 191 million acres (77.3 million hectares), which is an amount of land about the same size as Texas. In addition to protecting and managing America's public lands, the Forest Service also conducts forestry research and helps many state government and private forestry programs.

Glacier

A glacier is often called a river of ice. It is made of thick sheets of ice and snow. Glaciers slowly move downhill, scouring and smoothing the landscape.

WETLAND

A wetland, sometimes called riparian, is an area of land that usually has standing water for most of the year, like swamps or marshes. Many wetlands have been set aside as preserves for wildlife. Many kinds of birds and animals depend on this habitat for nesting, food, and shelter.

Above: Rock climbers undergo training sessions before attempting the two-day climb atop the formidable Grand Teton. This practice climb took place in Cascade Canyon.

Index